AFRICAN JOURNAL: A CHILD'S CONTINENT

North Africa

September 9, 1998

I begin this journal on my deathbed. I believe I may die this night behind the walls of the Medina, in a palace, in Morocco. I lie on sateen sheets in a queen-sized bed with a high fever. Blood as thick as tar is unleashed, emptying out the contents of what was the width and breadth of self. I hallucinate. Majestic, midnight black horses ridden by Arabian knights dance around these four walls, while monkeys shift-shape from man to hanuman, the magical Hindu monkey dressed in men's clothing, men's thoughts, men's deeds. Flies cover the plate of rice carried up the servants' staircase by Sophia; silently she comes to the landing that meets my bedroom door. "S'il vous plait, madam, a little rice is good".

Was it a dream or had I gone to the Hamam and watched, huddled, from a corner in the ancient underground sauna? Arms wrapped tightly around legs pulled close into chest. Eying the round European ladies. Through a steamy vale their naked bodies turn pink, as a pair of tiny hands scrub off dead skin with stiff, bristled brushes. I am told, yes, I was there. And did I board the bus that went up the steep mountain road? Rounding corners too close to its edge, to brave the Berber village? And see snake charmers and sway with ghosts as they rose from the mossy green and moist brown earth? That hides in the shadow of the Atlas Mountains?

The days turn to nights and back to days again before I recuperate. I wake, an empty vessel. Skin and bone hold together my body. I leave Marrakesh and the Medina to meet my family in Johannesburg. I will spend the next five years of my life surviving somewhere on the axis between heaven and hell.

*

When I wrote the lines above I really was afraid that I was dying. I'd gone to Morocco with friends to take photographs and an advanced course in the alternative medical field-Mind/Body Discipline-part of an on-going series of lectures I'd been attending for years. I woke the first night in Morocco with some non-specific illness, most likely dysentery, that lasted a week. My husband, Kevin, and two children, Jeannette and Octave, waited for me in our new home in Africa, the one I hadn't seen yet.

Kevin's computer software company had sent him to South Africa for a two-year stint, so we'd closed up the house in Oregon, packed every unnecessary object into oversized trunks and said goodbye cheerfully to the drizzle and gray skies of the US West Coast. We'd been to England for a year on a similar billeting, but this African posting was our first truly exotic one. And I was stupidly unprepared for it. Innocents Abroad. A quick read of Karen Blixen and Graham Greene-the only pertinent books on our shelves-did not, of course, introduce one to Africa, but to its colonial sins in beautiful prose.

I was still sick from the Morocco trip when the plane landed in Johannesburg and I joined my husband and children in a huge, rented house to the north. Stucco, yellow, pillared with French doors, I hadn't expected the opulence, but was even less prepared for the squatters' camps rammed against the perimeter of the property. Security guards with automatic rifles patrolled the massive stone walls. And there were four gardeners. All from Zimbabwe. No. This wasn't going to work, I knew immediately-this undilute outpost-despite the beauty of the country. I told my husband we couldn't stay, and when he insisted he had to for business reasons, I booked return flights for the children and myself. We'd been in Johannesburg ten days and it was the morning before our flight back to Oregon when I noticed one of the gardeners had gone missing. It was Isaac, the thin one, the one who'd instructed so carefully about the names of bushes and blooms.

"Where's Isaac?" I asked Joseph, his co-worker.
Joseph looked at his shoes, shredded Nikes, too big, the toes curled with age. "He's died, mum."
"Died?"
"He's died, mum. Of the sickness."
"What sickness, Joseph?"
"The one that gets them sicker and thinner. And terrible pain."
"But, he was here two days ago. Why didn't he tell me and we would have taken him to the hospital. What was the illness, Joseph? Its name?"
"The one where you die."
"Malaria?"
"No."
"TB?"
"No."
"Well it must have a name."
"No."

It took me twenty-four hours to find the illness with no name. The illness, that if you do say its name, might get you murdered. Or at the very least, ostracized. AIDS. Of course, Isaac had died of AIDS. I knew the virus had claimed many in sub-Saharan Africa but Isaac's death made me question how widespread the disease was, and how close. I asked the doctor at my son's school what was being done locally about HIV and AIDS. His answer shocked me.

"Mrs. Kew, in Zambia, for example, the national cry is, 'Everyone is either infected or affected by AIDS.' We in Johannesburg have a more difficult time with numbers because most lie if they have the illness. But do you know about the children?" he asked. "The adults who've died have left behind thousands of orphans. The AIDS orphans. If they are not on the street, or foster homes, one finds them in camps and mission schools throughout Zimbabwe, Botswana, Namibia, Mozambique and South Africa."

I cancelled the airplane tickets.
We were staying.
Whatever talents I had-photography and healing-I promised would be devoted to finding out where the orphans were and how they lived.

Joseph

The children's favorite photograph.

South Africa
October 5, 1998

I arrive to a raw, untamable land, of unsurpassed beauty and suppressed beating rage. The pendulum swings far out to the left and far out to the right, never resting at its center point, the place where calm is found. In Africa, I sense I will live in a world of seduction, felt as it rises from a geopathic force. A scorching energy claiming any and all whose internal compass is out of balance. I will view death, disease and dying and in the same instance see joy, compassion and generosity. I will come to know Africa is my home, my roots. Its people my people. Up from this ground comes a vine, circling my foot, calf and torso, to continue its spiraling motion towards heaven. I stand with arms open wide to embrace the cradle of mankind. I am re-connected to God and self. It matters not the color of my skin. For rushing through my veins is the remembrance of war, persecution and strife against a mighty and gentle people. I will come to understand: it is the children of Africa who will capture my heart and call me back to her, in my dreams.

My Africa

AIDS

Through her eyes
I am touched by Grace.

This small child's gaze,
dark as inkwells,
draws me into her soul.
An old soul
compassion emanating,
many life-times has she borne witness to.

She carries her tiny frame
wrapped around the core of her spiritual belief,
illumination;
a cross, centered,
holds her body in its rightful place.

I am in the presence of God.

I sense a knowing gratitude,
courage embodied for this mission
I am about to embark on.

She may die this day
or the next.
Peace rests in her face,
resolution,
for she knows she will return
into the waiting arms of her maker.

5.13.01

ANGEL

South Africa

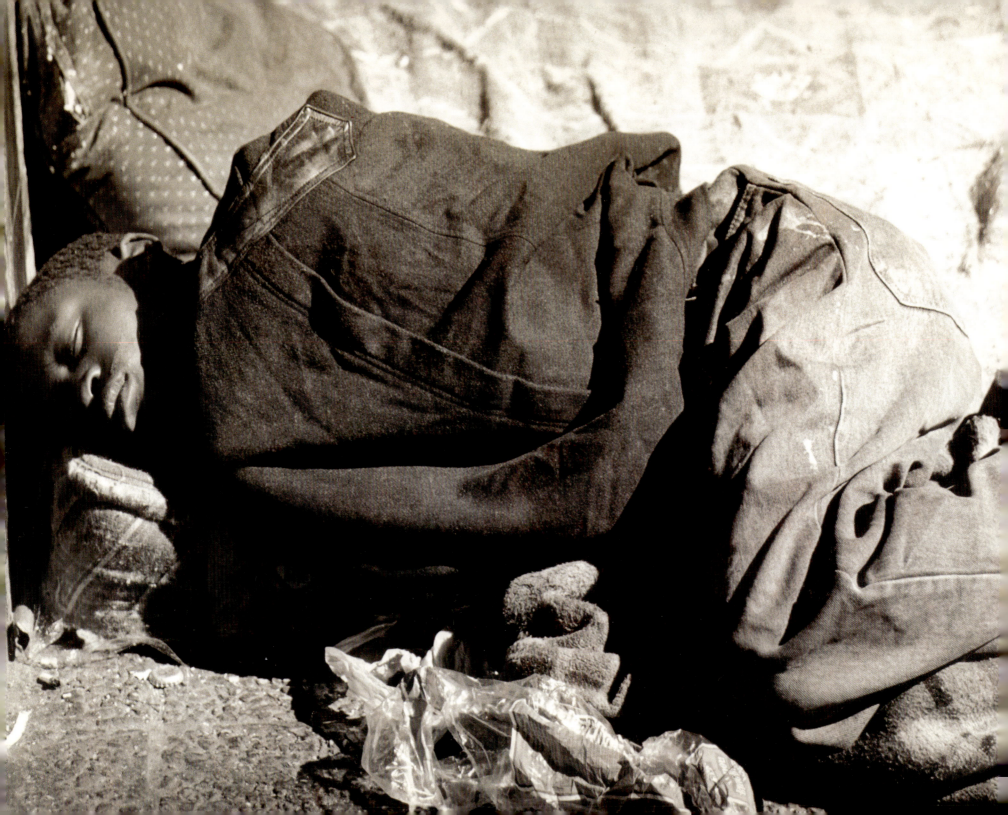

JOHANNESBURG

HOMELESS CHILDREN
Inner City, Johannesburg
June 24, 2001

Inside the iron bars of a makeshift classroom, some children play, some children sleep. I have entered the city of Hillbrow. Once home to the wealthy, it now stands in ruins. I walk into a war zone. Poverty, crime and retribution stiffen the air. Broken windows hold clothing lines hung heavy with graying garments. Dark concrete walls are permanently scarred with tribal graffiti.

Up from tattered mattresses flattened by years of daily use, leap two sleeping watchdogs, teenaged sentinels, keeping guard over the "babies" inside. "Power", introduces me to his attentive buddy, "Freedom". Eyeing my Nikon, he sizes it up in a moment for its street value. I hand over my new blue Nike knapsack filled with lenses, filters and film. Guards dropped, prideful expressions, and unspoken trust. in their stead, my self-appointed bodyguards usher me into the classroom.

I notice first the absence of toys within the dank, dark and barren room. A room hoping to form minds, hearts and creativity for the next generation of consumers and workforce. A room hoping to form teachers, politicians, physicians and artists. It is impossible to take photographs of the children stampeding over one another in hopes of being the first to be picked up. The first to be noticed, as each reaches out to be held. Power, Freedom and I, after promises to return, head to Toys "R" Us. Yes. Even in Africa.

We returned hours later with crayons, puzzles, blocks, balls all shapes and sizes and a plastic phone. The children are silent as each is given one gift. Mute. Nothing. Have I overdone it, played the "Lady Bountiful", embarrassing myself and them?

A little girl picks up the plastic telephone, methodically dials a phantom number and shouts into the receiver, my name. A roar of glee. The room erupts.

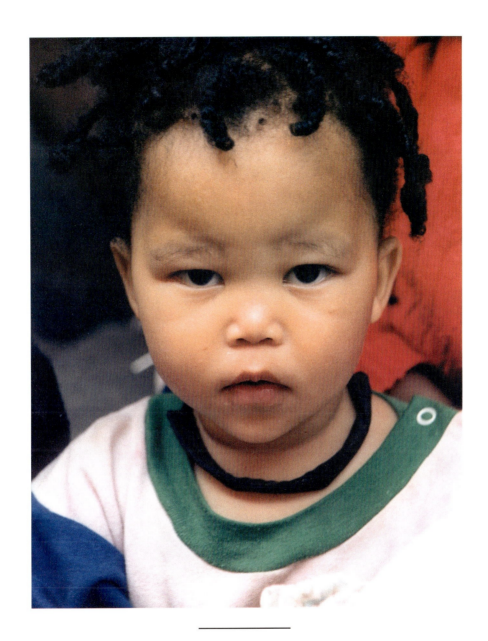

Rose

Freedom

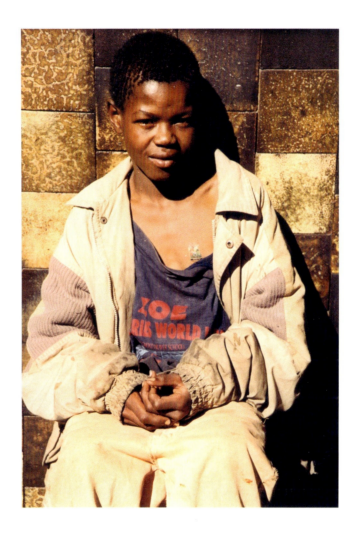

Power

Ishmael

Squatters Camp, Soweto
August 17, 2001

It is early morning outside Johannesburg. I am in the squatters' camp. The day is dark, the temperature only slightly above freezing. The camp is a labyrinth of muddy crossroads. It is a maze of endless twists and turns, row upon row of metal sheeting, barbed wire fences, discarded cars, tires. Unprepared, I've worn flip-flops; it's hard to find dry footing in the rain and raw sewage.

The brown, wet streets frame the corrugated tin-walled and tin-roofed dwellings. Inside the structures, two rooms house up to 24 children, boys in one room, girls in the other. Rain drips through the seam of the roofline. The children are barefoot. The only warmth in the house comes from their faces, a steamy aura.

Huddled around a useless stove, they tell stories of watching mother and father die from an unknown sickness. Agonizingly long, slow and painful deaths are witnessed. Joshua, Gift and Grace recount tales of how, at the end, parents were carted off in a wheelbarrow to be propped alongside the many others awaiting a proper burial.

The graveyards are full. Grace is worried that her mother will never be buried. To go to heaven, Grace's mother must have the proper ritual: the purification wash and anointing, the nighttime vigil when the next of kin guard and bless the body. There is no one left in her family to perform the ancient burial rite.

Unlike the children in rural South Africa, the children of Soweto have some understanding of the AIDS virus, though their notions are part myth, part lie. Many South Africans, including the President, Thabo Mbeki, deny any link between HIV and AIDS. The children have been told, the older children at least, that if they suspect they are infected, tell no one. An admission to the disease means certain alienation and possible murder.

Joshua

"In sub-Saharan Africa 470,000 children die every year from AIDS."
Joyce Maxwell, CNN

Grace

"In Africa, the greatest gift a husband gives his wife is their child".
Traditional African proverb

Gift

Orphanage in Soweto

"New shoes"

Domo

"HIV and the AIDS is real. Really, really, really, don't be silly, HIV and the AIDS is real."
African children's song

Dharma

ZIMBABWE

The children counter in Emmanuel's village.

Zimbabwe

September 20, 2001

It's six o'clock in the morning. The day is cold in Johannesburg; my breath is visible as I pull tightly the outer layer of my clothing. Winter has arrived. I board the S.A.A. flight bound for Victoria Falls. Emmanuel, my driver, will meet me tomorrow morning in the hotel lobby.

The Victoria Falls Hotel sits high above its namesake. The widest waterfall in the world stretches to bridge the distance between Zimbabwe and Zambia. Flamingo-pink alabaster exterior walls frame black shutters, windows and doors. Tall, polished white columns hold long, low, patios that open up under the shade of the Acacia tree. Entering into the foyer, trophies gaze down with frozen expressions as antique photographs of exotic birds, spotted leopards and white-faced monkeys stare back at me. Skins warm the ebony floor in shades of cream and chocolate. The "bush donkey" is the name the locals have given to the zebra. Black and white stripes melt into one another along the grassy landscape that once was the breadbasket for Africa. Years of starvation, murder, death and disease, leave a trail of bloodshed staining the ground where tall sweet corn and sunflowers grew.

A funeral procession passes by. I am told this happens throughout the days. It is said, if a family member does not attend this funeral then he must be responsible for the death. He will be charged accordingly. The absent family member is the guilty party. Superstition forces people to leave jobs behind. A day or a week's loss of pay is guaranteed for those making the long journey back home. By foot, bus or taxi they travel to honor their dead. They are afraid if they do not arrive in time for the burial, additional family members will fall under an evil spell. Someone else will die.

Emmanuel takes me into his village. His village has a great number of the AIDS affected orphans. We drive slowly along the side of a one-roomed schoolhouse. The building is creamy stucco with cobalt blue wooden door and window frames. On the playground there is a grid made up of rocks. Each different row indicates one grade level. Students choose the appropriate line before classes will begin. An old man sits on a chair and counts to see which new child is absent, possibly dead from the virus. The children wear uniforms without shoes. Dewy footprints are visible on cold sand.

Prince Charles, named for his quick wit, and his sister, Anna, sit on the ground playing with a younger cousin. She is very ill. White spots cover her arms and legs. Prince Charles' mother died from the disease. His father disappeared soon after. They are lucky to have a grandmother. Most children living in Zimbabwe are left without parents. Most are caregivers for younger siblings.

The grandmother carries a bundle on top of her head: a yellow and white piece of fabric ties everything in place. There is an infant nestled between her large breasts. A young child peeks from behind her, tiny fingers squeeze tight a piece of tattered hem as it unfolds at the bottom of 'Grand's' skirt. Far behind a boy carries the family water. He fetches it, daily. Seven kilometers away. Prince Charles' younger cousin does not speak anymore. She is the latest victim of the belief, "If one sleeps with a virgin, you will be cured of AIDS."

"By 2010 African orphans may exceed 40 million"
UNAID

Prince Charles

11 million AIDS affected orphans in sub-Saharan Africa.
CBS News

11.8 million children live, in the United Kingdom.
UK census report

Anna

"Bush donkey" with egret.

Before leaving the village I asked Lilian. "Is there anything you need from the US"?
"Yes," answered Grandmother. "Could I please have toys and shoes for the children, and please may I have a dress?
A red dress, I want to wear it for church."

MOZAMBIQUE

Painted house

Refugees From Mozambique

October 12, 2001

It's late. Three thirty in the afternoon. And hot. As we drive into the camps, the children scatter and hide. Dust flies from the rear wheels. I have caught a brief glimpse of the children despite their reticence. The color of their skin is that of warm, red-brown mud after the rains have dried. They are afraid and won't approach because I'm white.

We are in the camps of Mozambique, the camps on the border with South Africa. We have driven, but the refugees must walk through the Kruger National Game Reserve to reach the compound. Many die, killed by lions and hippos. The land in the camps is bare for hundreds of meters in all directions. The Mozambicans have cut all the trees in a mile-wide swath around their mud and thatch dwellings. Only sticks remain. It is their fear of snakes that makes them strip the land, justified by the number and the deadly venom of the local species.

One by one, faces appear from behind huts, discarded wheelbarrows and empty boxes. I hear giggles as the shy children need to touch my hair, the leopard-patterned frame of my glasses.

Could they please look through the lens of the camera? Could they please take a picture?

I take a stick to draw in the sand: people, houses, birds and animals the children have never seen. I ask some of the older children if they understand what AIDS is. Most respond that it's a "killer". Would they agree to be tested? No. Why not? "If I have it then I know I will die and my friends will not speak to me anymore." "I may be killed."

It is the first time ever, in this compound, that I have seen paint. Paint on square houses. Pale ochre with terracotta patterns. A painted home is so rare that the missionary assures me this is a sign of permanence. This means that even though years of war, poverty and floods have left them wary, the Mozambicans are not without hope.

Lucky

Ten percent of the world's people live in Africa, but it is home to 90 percent of the world's HIV-infected children.

Maxwell

"Best Friends"

Samuel & Christmas

Lioness seen in the Kruger.

Charles & Joy

"Do not stigmatize people with AIDS. Show them care, support and, above all, love. It is your duty to be human."
Nelson Mandela

Isaac

Ezico

Christina wants to be a nurse when she grows up.

Christina and her Brother Abraham

BOTSWANA

Botswana

November 20, 2001

The temperature is well above 100 degrees Fahrenheit in the Kalahari, not a shade tree anywhere. I smell my skin roast, a strange smell, not bad only odd. It's not the scorpions, snakes and spiders that are most troublesome. But the goats, the cows, the donkeys-noisemakers-trampling everything. Such a clatter, even though we've left the tar road far behind and now live in deep, red, endless sand. The truck breaks down, is stuck, trapped, between blowing sand and smothering heat. Botswana is the wealthiest country in Southern Africa, but the virus knows no difference between rich and poor. My new friends, Conrad and Anna have devoted their lives to the children with AIDS in this region. I wonder if I am up to it, I haven't their courage in this heat.

The children here are of a distinctive color, shape and size: high cheekbones, light skin, dust-colored, cropped hair, thin bodies, strong white teeth. "The Basharwa" is the name the new government has issued them, like blankets. They are the discarded, the outcast. These rich, loving, easy people are an embarrassment to Botswanans. Yet, these are the cattle herders of the Kalahari. A shepherd watches 10,000 of the longhorn stock and knows when a single animal is missing. He knows each cow by sight. Both children and adults have the skill.

The children are in constant pain from the AIDS virus. They're given beer to help them sleep. I show them how to wash their hands and faces using sand. We make a game of it. We use body language, charades, as neither speaks the others' native tongue.

The sadness here is overwhelming. I stay in the sun too long. There's little water. By evening, I am dehydrated and cannot move.

I lie in my tent trying unsuccessfully to escape the heat. The tent is built on a metal frame on the roof of the "Bakkie", a Toyota SUV. The dark, green canvas with zippered windows and door unfolds; and then ties snugly to the roof of the "Bakkie". An ingenious invention, this snail-like hybrid, it affords no breeze this night in Botswana.

I hear the sounds of the ritual trance dance. It's the night of the full moon. The herders have prepared for the dance the previous night. I hear songs, screams: this is the night to exorcise demons. Or to heal. This night the children heal me. The children are not allowed to attend the trance dance. So instead, hundreds of the smallest surround the Bakkie and sing. The pitch, rhyme, rhythm, the perfect harmony, it is the sound only children can make. They call to me, singing "the one with the bird-colored eyes."

I have not been able to say goodbye. The following morning, a truck takes me on a delirious ride to the border of Botswana and South Africa. I remember nothing of the five-hour ride.

Sphanzambla

Young cattle herder of the Kalahari.

Okavango Delta, Botswana.
A large black-maned lion, spotted while driving to
the Basharwa out-post.

It is estimated 1 in 5 carry the virus

NAMIBIA

Namibia

March 14th and 15th 2002

I arrive at Windhoek Airport in the capital of Namibia, and rent a Toyota 4X4 equipped with a cell phone and maps. I head west towards Sossusvlei. The road ahead is a straight uninterrupted line edging a carpet of tiny yellow flowers. I see red boulders far in the distance. There is a warm sweetness coming off the desert floor and the sky is blue. It is the end of the rainy season in Namibia and out of the city limits the blacktop quickly disappears into loose gravel. Signposts are far apart and few, swept away by torrential rains. Liquid evaporates in the blink of an eye leaving behind parched orange and brown earth. Trees lie low, bent, in the shape of a bow, forever seeking vanishing puddles of water. There is an absence of other vehicles. I see more donkeys, Black-backed Jackal and cattle than people or cars. In and out goes the signal for the radio. I switch it off as my eyes rest on the gas gauge. It is stuck in the "Full" position. With four hours drive behind me, and one to go before I reach the Desert Wilderness Lodge, I pull over and look at a map. I find the small symbol for a gas station. I am at the center point, halfway between the station and tonight's accommodation.

The truck's wheels bump over cattle guards placed in the dirt to keep cattle in and prey out. Birds are singing, donkeys walk lazily down the side of the road, tails swishing at flies. I drive too fast around a sharp bend. The road drops. There, in front of me, is an Impala. I swerve, out of control. The rear wheels skate sideways to the left then lock right. Aiming for a three-foot embankment, I struggle with the steering wheel and lunge forward, hitting a tremendous boulder headfirst. The truck flips. My head smashes against the window.

A strong wind blows. The rain will follow shortly. "Is there anyone there?" I am sure I have heard a sound. The cold is unbearable. I have a dream. A lion. He sits pressed up against the chassis of the truck. Patiently he waits for morning. God and the Devil are at war. There is a struggle deep within my body. I am stripped, exposed, vulnerable. An animal on a nightly walk bumps the back of the truck. Is it the lion? No. No. Only the truck emergency flashers. On. Off. I turn on the headlights and see nothing in the road ahead, in the distance, visible to the light's edge.

I wake to the black of night. I taste blood and gasoline at the back of my throat. Unfastening the seatbelt, barefoot, I step up and over the stick shift onto snowflake fragments of glass. I turn on the interior light of the vehicle and dial the three numbers for emergency on the cell phone and am unprepared for the recording, a metallic English accent advising, "You are presently out of network range." I push against the truck's horn: dot dot dot-dash dash dash-dot dot dot. The sound is lost in the vast open space. Wrapping the map around me for warmth and stuffing a T-Shirt into the crack of the broken window, I pass out.

Two hours later I regain consciousness. This time, though, the Southern Cross is visible in the night sky, and a bowl of stars reaches from horizon to horizon, 180 degrees. This gives me courage to exit the truck. Hoisting myself through the driver's side door of the up-ended truck, my ribs ache and blood marks a thin path down my cheek. I cannot stop shivering. The blow to my head has made the simplest reasoning impossible: Which is the greater distance? The thirteen kilometers back to the farm or the thirty-six kilometers to the village ahead, Solitude? A village named Solitude? Is thirteen greater than thirty-six? So many threes. The name Solitude frightens me, though I cannot order the numbers properly, so in the end it is a freak intuition that sets me off in the right direction.

I lick the blood from my hands and face and bury my urine in the sand. Futile attempts at safety because both are tart scents to the predator, delicious tracks. I am in leopard country. The leopard is everywhere in the Namibian Desert, like the street stray of Rome. During the night, three sets of prints have circled the truck: a donkey's, the Impala, and the third, a cat's. A small one, but that's no comfort. "One must never leave the vehicle," the embassy representative had cautioned. But in Africa, all rules are broken. I've got to walk. Soon the heat will come. The temperature will rise fifty degrees in the first hour; I carry with me three figs, a bottle of "Rescue Remedy," and my passport. No water. My camera crushed. The passport is in case I do not make it back. My children will at least be able to identify the body.

*

Thirty-two hours later, I am in the Windhoek Hospital. A male baboon had followed me for some hours on the road, his yellow teeth and gray coat appearing now behind, now above a boulder ahead.

I heard the noise the birds make when a leopard is close by, and a donkey passed once. Otherwise, there had been no cars, nothing, until, against all odds, a hunter, inoculating sheep in a field, spotted me, gave me water and arranged my transport to the hospital.

My thoughts about Africa, and myself in Africa, had changed during this long night and day before I was rescued. Throughout my journeys to the orphanages these past years, I've felt sympathy, but this new feeling I had had, alone in the desert, was something else. Terror, hunger, thirst, despair in a drowning mix. Perhaps I needed the accident to fully comprehend the daily tragedies and triumphs these children face. I made a promise to the children that night. If I survived, I would show their pictures. I'd speak of their courage. I would write a book that raised awareness about their plight, their gentleness, their joy, their sorrow. If I ever made it back home, I would remember my walk forward through a Child's Continent.

Chellie Kew
Author/Photographer

As a professional model in the New York City fashion industry, Chellie Kew started her photography career in front of the camera. The results of Chellie's modeling work have been portrayed in a variety of well-known women's publications, including Cosmopolitan, Mademoiselle, Seventeen, Co-Ed and Teen magazines. While living in South Africa, Chellie's work behind the camera continued to blossom while on numerous photo adventures resulting in raw and upfront images of African children and wildlife in Botswana, Zimbabwe, Namibia, Mozambique and South Africa.

Prior to moving to South Africa Chellie ran Kew Garden, a private, home-based facility specializing in the area of skincare, Cranial Fluid Dynamics, Acupuncture/Acupressure, Kinesology, Reflexology and Mudras—commonly referred to as an Ontological process. Chellie is now applying her accomplished skills as a photographer, and her holistic approach to health and the pursuit of well being, to the young and innocent of sub-Saharan Africa.

Founder, The Q Fund 4 AIDS

Moses

Acknowledgements

The orphans of Southern Africa for allowing me to capture a glimpse of Grace held within each child. I would like to thank my family and friends for their moral support and my husband Kevin for his encouragement and support with this project. To the missionaries Conrad, Johan and Anna, for those times when my path was thwarted by unforeseen obstacles, it was their kind words that kept me moving forward. I came to understand the meaning of the word devotion, as I witnessed their work with children suffering from AIDS in Africa.

Thanks to my brother Parker Wallman for having the patience and creativity to produce this book, and to Char Liske, Executive Vice President, at Dynagraphics, many thanks. David and Denise Tokoph, for the generosity they have shown me. Jeremy Peele, who ran the "Half-Iron Man" marathon in the name of The "Q" Fund. To Michael and Martha Nesbitt for being the first family friends to contribute towards this fund. Fiona Eberts and Eric Meier for contributions. Anna and Victor, who constantly cared for my work and me.

I would like to thank Beata Marino and Dr. Paula Kilpatrick for putting my broken body back together again with healing hands and heart. And last but not least, to my Mother, Joan Blake who believed in my true talent as a photographer and writer.

Dedication

To my children Jeannette and Octavio, through them I was taught the meaning of how to give and receive unconditional love.

Photographs, graphics and stories copyright © 2003 by Michelle Blake Kew
All rights reserved. No portion of this book may be reproduced or utilized in any form, or by any electronic, mechanical, or other means without the prior written permission of the publisher.

Published by The Q Fund.
Cover and interior design: Parker Wallman
Writing assistant: Tia Wallman
Printed by Dynagraphics Inc.
ISBN 0-9729909-0-9

Some names have been changed to protect the privacy of the children.